Learning to Read, Step by Step!

Ready to Read   **Preschool–Kindergarten**
• big type and easy words • rhyme and rhythm • picture clues
For children who know the alphabet and are eager to begin reading.

Reading with Help   **Preschool–Grade 1**
• basic vocabulary • short sentences • simple stories
For children who recognize familiar words and sound out new words with help.

Reading on Your Own   **Grades 1–3**
• engaging characters • easy-to-follow plots • popular topics
For children who are ready to read on their own.

Reading Paragraphs   **Grades 2–3**
• challenging vocabulary • short paragraphs • exciting stories
For newly independent readers who read simple sentences with confidence.

Ready for Chapters   **Grades 2–4**
• chapters • longer paragraphs • full-color art
For children who want to take the plunge into chapter books but still like colorful pictures.

STEP INTO READING® is designed to give every child a successful reading experience. The grade levels are only guides; children will progress through the steps at their own speed, developing confidence in their reading. The F&P Text Level on the back cover serves as another tool to help you choose the right book for your child.

Remember, a lifetime love of reading starts with a single step!

For my nieces, Kirsten and Erica
—J.M.

For my dearest cubs, Leonardo and Lorenzo
—F.T.

With thanks to Dr. Thomas R. Holtz, Jr., Department of Geology, University of Maryland, for his assistance in the preparation of this book.

Text copyright © 1985 by Joyce Milton
Revised text copyright © 2014 by Kent Milton
Cover art and interior illustrations copyright © 2014 by Franco Tempesta

Visit us on the Web!
StepIntoReading.com
randomhouse.com/kids

Educators and librarians, for a variety of teaching tools, visit us at
RHTeachersLibrarians.com

Library of Congress Cataloging-in-Publication Data
Milton, Joyce, author.
Dinosaur days / Joyce Milton ; illustrated by Franco Tempesta. — First edition.
    pages cm. — (Step into reading. Step 3)
Summary: "Illus. in full color. Difficult dinosaur names are simplified with phonics."
—Provided by publisher.
ISBN 978-0-385-37923-6 (trade pbk.) — ISBN 978-0-375-97338-3 (lib. bdg.) —
ISBN 978-0-307-97870-7 (ebook)
1. Dinosaurs—Juvenile literature. I. Tempesta, Franco, illustrator. II. Title.
QE861.5.M55 2014 567.9—dc23 2013044052

Printed in the United States of America
10 9 8 7 6 5 4

This book has been officially leveled by using the F&P Text Level Gradient™ Leveling System.

STEP INTO READING®

3

STEP

A SCIENCE READER

Dinosaur Days

by Joyce Milton

illustrated by Franco Tempesta

Random House 🏠 New York

Sometimes people find bones
of ancient animals.
Some of these bones
are from dinosaurs.

The bones are like
parts of a puzzle.
When they are put together,
you can see
what a dinosaur looked like.

The word *dinosaur* looks hard,

but it is really easy to say.

Say: DIE-nuh-sor.

Dinosaur means "fearfully great lizard."

Millions of years ago
the world belonged
to dinosaurs.

In the days of the dinosaurs,
there were no people.
No dogs or cats.
No horses or cows.

What animals were there?

Turtles.

Crocodiles.

Fish.

Dragonflies.

The world was warmer
than today,
and very wet in some places.

One of the very first dinosaurs
was *Panphagia*
(pan-FAYG-ee-uh).

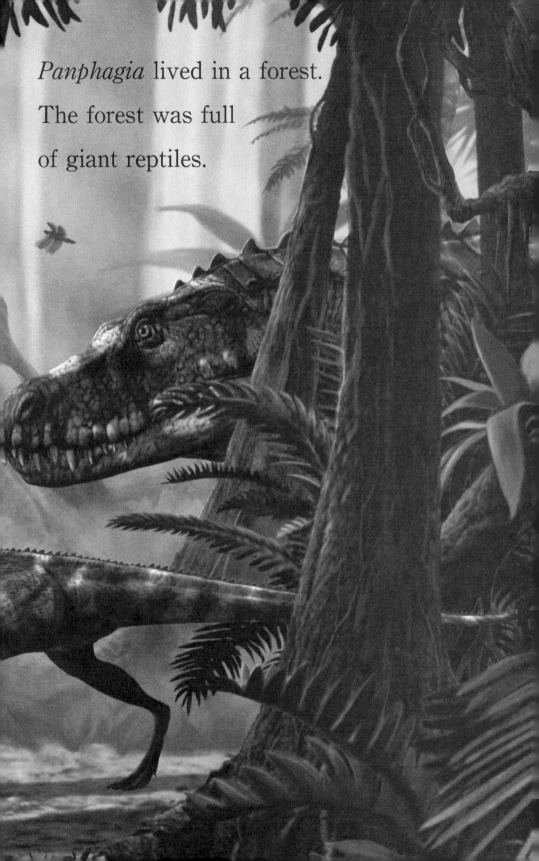

Panphagia lived in a forest.
The forest was full
of giant reptiles.

When these giants got hungry,
they came after *Panphagia*.
SNAP! went the giants' jaws.
SNAP! SNAP!
Then *Panphagia*
ran away as fast as it could
on its strong back legs.

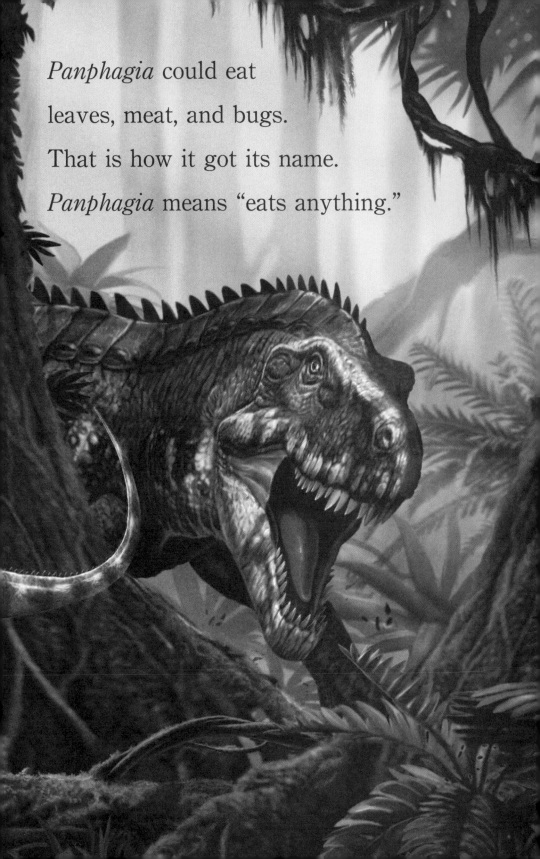

Panphagia could eat
leaves, meat, and bugs.
That is how it got its name.
Panphagia means "eats anything."

Panphagia was a small dinosaur.

It was about the size of a turkey.

Dinosaurs came in many sizes.

Some were small like *Panphagia*.

Some were big.

And some

were very, very big.

One of the biggest
was *Argentinosaurus*
(ar-jun-TEE-nuh-SAW-rus).

This dinosaur was
as big as a house,
longer than three buses,
and as heavy
as thirteen elephants!

The name *Argentinosaurus*
means "lizard from Argentina."
That is the country
where its bones were found.
Argentinosaurus ate plants.
Lots of them!

Other dinosaurs hunted
for meat to eat.
One meat-eater
was named *Mapusaurus*
(MAH-poo-SAW-rus).

A grown-up *Argentinosaurus*
was too big for most
meat-eaters to hunt.
But a baby *Argentinosaurus*
would be the right size
for a snack.

This dinosaur was not big
and it was not fast.
It could not run and hide.
But it did not need to!

Its back was protected
by bony plates.
Its name was *Scelidosaurus*
(skeh-LIH-duh-SAW-rus).
It was one of the first
armored dinosaurs.

Not all kinds of dinosaurs
lived at the same time.
Early dinosaurs
like *Scelidosaurus*
died out.
New kinds
took their place.

Some of the newer dinosaurs
looked a little like ducks.
They are called
duck-billed dinosaurs.

This duck-billed dinosaur
is called *Edmontosaurus*
(ed-MON-tuh-SAW-rus).

Edmontosaurus had lots of teeth.
Almost one thousand of them!
It used its teeth
to mash up plants.

This is *Tyrannosaurus rex*
(tie-RAN-uh-SAW-rus REX).
It had some of the biggest teeth
of all dinosaurs.

Its teeth were as long as bananas
and very strong.
The word *rex* means "king."
This dinosaur was the king
of the hunters.
What did it hunt?
Other dinosaurs!

Some dinosaurs
had ways to keep safe
from *Tyrannosaurus rex*.
This dinosaur
had hard plates on its back.
The plates were like armor.
When danger was near,
it just sat tight.

The name of this dinosaur
is *Ankylosaurus*
(an-KEE-luh-SAW-rus).
Ankylosaurus also had
a strong tail.
It could swing its tail
like a club.

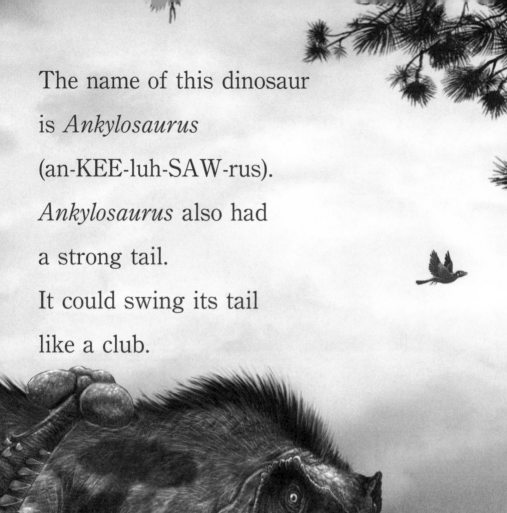

This dinosaur
used its sharp horns
for fighting.
When it charged,
everyone got out of the way!

Its name is *Triceratops*
(try-SER-uh-tops).
That means "three-horned face."

We know some amazing things
about dinosaurs.
We know that some
had feathers like birds!
We know that some were colored
black and red and white and brown.
But we do not know the colors
of most of them.

Microraptor

Sinosauropteryx

Anchiornis

We also know
how dinosaurs were born.
They hatched from eggs,
just like baby birds!

Some dinosaur eggs
were big . . .
even bigger than a football.
But some were only the size
of a potato.

This dinosaur
is named *Citipati*
(CHEE-tee-pah-tee).
The mother and father
made nests in the sand.
The mother laid many eggs.
The mother and father took turns
sitting on the eggs.
Their feathers
helped keep the eggs warm.

When the babies were born,
they were very small.
Much, much smaller
than their parents.
You could hold
a baby *Citipati*
in your hands.

In the days of the dinosaurs,
strange animals
lived in the sea.
They were real-life sea monsters.
Some of these monsters
looked like dinosaurs.

But they were not dinosaurs.
They are called plesiosaurs
(PLEE-zee-uh-SORS).
They had long necks.
They reached into the water
to catch fish.

Other strange animals
flew in the air.
One of these animals
was *Pteranodon*
(tuh-RAN-uh-don).
Its body was no bigger
than a turkey's.
But its wings were as wide
as the wings of a small plane.

Pteranodon flew far out to sea.
It rested on the tops of waves.
When it took off,
it soared on the wind
like a glider.

The days of the dinosaurs
lasted a very long time.
Millions and millions of years.
Then a time came
when an asteroid
smashed into the earth.
An asteroid is a
giant rock from space.

The darkness and the cold
meant most dinosaurs
could not find food to eat.

But one kind of
little feathered flying dinosaur
survived.

We still have these dinosaurs today.

They are called birds!

So the dinosaur days go on.